Cadmium

I0473880

U.S. Department of Labor

Occupational Safety and Health Administration

OSHA 3136-06R
2004

Contents

Introduction

Cadmium, a naturally occurring element found in the earth's crust, was discovered in 1817, but was not used commercially until the end of the 19th century. This soft, silver-white metal was first used in paint pigments and as a substitute for tin in World War I. Today, about three-fourths of cadmium is used as an electrode component in alkaline batteries, with the remainder used in pigments, coatings, and platings and as a stabilizer for plastics.

Workers in many industries face potential exposure to cadmium. The potential for exposure is highest among workers in electroplating, metal machining, plastics, ceramics, paint, and welding operations. The main exposure routes are through inhalation of dust and fumes and the incidental ingestion of dust from contaminated hands, food, or cigarettes.

Workers may also be exposed to cadmium from the smelting and refining of metals or from air in industrial plants that manufacture batteries, coatings, or plastics. The Agency for Toxic Substances and Disease Registry estimates that more than 500,000 workers in the United States face exposure to cadmium each year.

How OSHA protects workers exposed to cadmium

The primary and most serious adverse health effects of long-term exposure to cadmium include kidney dysfunction, lung cancer, and prostate cancer. Cadmium may cause local skin or eye irritation and can affect long-term health if inhaled or ingested. Workers face a greater danger of cadmium exposure from inhalation than from ingestion. Exposure to cadmium that may be dangerous to life or health may occur in jobs in which workers are exposed to cadmium dust or fumes, where they heat compounds or surfaces that contain cadmium, or where workers weld or cut with materials or solders that contain cadmium.

OSHA moved to protect workers exposed to cadmium more than 30 years ago when it adopted the American National Standards Institute's (ANSI) threshold limit values (TLVs) for cadmium as a national consensus standard under the authority of the Occupational Safety and Health Act of 1970, Section 6(a) in 1971. In 1992, OSHA reduced the exposure limits after a quantitative risk assessment and a long-term evaluation of epidemiological studies of lung cancer and renal dysfunction among workers and animal studies. The revised exposure limits were published in the Federal Register (Title 29 CFR, Part 1910.1027) and took effect on December 14, 1992.

The full OSHA standard relating to cadmium (applicable to general industry, agriculture, and maritime) is found at 29 CFR 1910.1027. This booklet should not be used as a substitute for the full regulatory requirements of the cadmium standard. The construction industry has a separate cadmium standard, found in 29 CFR 1926.1127.

Exposure limits for cadmium

There are three exposure limits an employer must observe under the OSHA cadmium standard. The first is the action level, or AL, which is defined as the airborne level of cadmium that creates a need for airborne exposure monitoring, a medical surveillance program for employees who are at or above the AL on 30 or more days per year, and the provision of a respirator to any employee that requests one. The second limit is the Permissible Exposure Limit, or PEL, which defines the limit to which an employee may be exposed to cadmium in the workplace. The third limit level is known as a Separate Engineering Control Air Limit, or SECAL, and may be one of several specific and unique exposure limits that apply to select and defined industries and processes. The employer must achieve the PEL through engineering controls and work practices in all industries not designated with a separate SECAL.

The action level

The action level for workplace exposure to cadmium is 2.5 micrograms per cubic meter of air (2.5 $\mu g/m^3$) calculated as an 8-hour time-weighted average (TWA) exposure.

The PEL

The PEL is a time-weighted average concentration that must not be exceeded during any 8-hour work shift of a 40-hour work week. The standard sets a PEL of 5 micrograms of cadmium per cubic meter of air (5 $\mu g/m^3$) for all cadmium compounds, dust, and fumes.

The SECALs

The SECAL is a separate exposure limit to be achieved in specified processes and workplaces where it is not possible to achieve the PEL of 5 μg/m^3 through engineering and work practices alone. The SECAL for cadmium is 15 μg/m^3 or 50 μg/m^3, depending on the processes involved. The employer covered by the SECAL is required to achieve that limit by engineering and work practice controls to the extent feasible and to protect employees from exposures above the PEL by any combination of compliance methods, including engineering and work practice controls and respirators.

The industries that have separate SECALs identified for specific processes include nickel cadmium battery production, zinc/cadmium refining, pigment and stabilizer manufacturing, lead smelting, and plating.

The SECAL is set at 50 μg/m^3 for the following industries and processes:

- Nickel cadmium battery industry
  Plate making, plate preparation process

- Zinc/cadmium refining
  Cadmium refining, casting melting, oxide production, sinter plant

- Pigment manufacturing
  Calcine, crushing, milling, and blending

- Stabilizer production
  Cadmium oxide charging, crushing, drying, and blending

- Lead smelting
  Sinter plant, blast furnace, baghouse, and yard area

The SECAL is set at 15 μg/m^3 for the following industries and processes:

- Nickel cadmium battery industry
  All processes not identified above

- Pigment manufacturing
  All processes not identified above

- Plating manufacturing
  Mechanical plating

Communicating cadmium hazards to employees

Employees must be made aware of the dangers associated with exposure to cadmium in the workplace. The employer must comply with the requirements of the OSHA Hazard Communication Standard (29 CFR 1910.1200), including the placement of warning signs and labels in visible locations, access to material safety data sheets (MSDS), and providing appropriate employee training.

Warning signs must be displayed in regulated areas and in all approaches to regulated areas. (A regulated area is defined as the area in which an employee may face exposure to cadmium at levels above the PEL.) The signs must be illuminated, cleaned, and maintained so that the legend is readily visible, and they must include the following words:

- Danger
- Cadmium
- Cancer hazard
- Can cause lung and kidney disease
- Authorized personnel only
- Respirators required in this area

Shipping and storage containers that contain cadmium, cadmium compounds, or cadmium-contaminated clothing, equipment, waste, scrap, or debris must be labeled with the following information:

- Danger
- Contains cadmium
- Cancer hazard
- Avoid creating dust
- Can cause lung and kidney disease

Installed cadmium products must have a visible label or other indication that cadmium is present, where feasible.

Employee training

Employees must receive training prior to or at the time of their initial assignment to a position that involves potential exposure to cadmium and at least annually thereafter. Required training elements include:

- Explanation of the health hazards associated with cadmium exposure (See Appendix A of the cadmium standard at 29 CFR 1910.1027).

- Information about where and how cadmium is used, stored, and released at the worksite, including processes or operations that involve potential cadmium exposure, especially above the PEL.

- Explanation of engineering controls and work practices for the employee's job assignment to control exposure to cadmium associated with the employee's job assignment.

- Description of measures employees can take to protect themselves from cadmium exposure, such as modification of smoking, personal hygiene precautions, and appropriate work practices.

- Explanation of emergency procedures.

- Information on the purpose, selection, fitting, use, and limitations of personal protective equipment.

- Explanation of the medical surveillance program.

- Make a copy of the cadmium standard and its appendices readily available and provide employees with a copy of the standard if requested.

- Informing employees of their rights of access to records.

The employer must ensure that employees understand that they are prohibited from eating, drinking, smoking, chewing tobacco or gum, or applying cosmetics of any kind in regulated areas. This also includes a prohibition on carrying or storing these materials or items in a regulated area.

The employer must make information about the company training program available to the Assistant Secretary of Labor for Occupational Safety and Health or the Director of the National Institute for Occupational Safety and Health upon request.

Requirements for air monitoring for cadmium

If your business or workplace has the potential to expose employees to cadmium, the first step is to determine whether that exposure will be at or above the action level of 2.5 μg/m^3. Levels of exposure are measured by taking breathing zone air samples that reflect an employee's regular, daily TWA exposure over an eight-hour period. The monitoring method and analysis must have an accuracy rate of not less than plus or minus 25 percent with a confidence level of 95 percent.

The breathing zone samples must be taken for every employee on each shift, for each job classification, in each work area. Where several employees perform the same job tasks, in the same job classification, on the same shift, in the same work area, for the same duration, and levels of cadmium exposures are similar, the employer may sample a representative fraction of employees instead of all employees. Those selected for sampling are expected to have the highest exposure levels.

If air monitoring shows that employees are exposed at or above the action level, periodic monitoring must be performed at least every six months. If periodic air monitoring shows levels of exposure below the action level and a repeat test at least seven days later also shows levels below the action level, the employer may discontinue the semi-annual air monitoring for those employees whose exposures are represented by such monitoring.

If new equipment is added, raw materials are changed, new personnel are hired, work practices and final products are altered that may result in additional employees being exposed to cadmium at or above the action level, additional monitoring must be performed. If, at any time, the employer has reason to suspect that exposure to cadmium may increase and employees already exposed to cadmium at or above the action level will be exposed above the PEL, additional air monitoring should be undertaken.

If the employer has "objective data", which means information that demonstrates that a specific product, material, or process involving cadmium cannot release dust or fumes in concentrations at or above the action level based on an industry-wide study or laboratory product test results that closely resemble conditions in the employer's facilities, then the employer may rely on this data instead of implementing initial monitoring as described above.

Notifying employees of monitoring results

Within 15 days after the receipt of the air monitoring results, each affected employee must be notified of these results individually and in writing. The results must also be posted where all affected employees can view them. Employees exposed to cadmium above the PEL must be informed in writing that the PEL has been exceeded, along with a written explanation of the corrective actions being taken by the employer to reduce the employee exposure level to or below the PEL.

Mechanical ventilation

If mechanical ventilation is used to control exposure, measurements that demonstrate the effectiveness of the system in controlling exposure, such as capture velocity, duct velocity, or static pressure, must be made as necessary, to maintain the system's effectiveness. Any change in production processes or controls that might increase cadmium exposure requires the effectiveness of the ventilation system to be reevaluated within five working days of the change.

If air is recirculated from exhaust ventilation into the workplace, the system must be equipped with a high efficiency filter and be monitored periodically to ensure effectiveness.

Requirements for a compliance program

In any workplace or business that experiences exposure levels above the PEL or SECAL, a written compliance program must be established and implemented to reduce employee exposure to or below the PEL by means of engineering and work practice controls. If engineering and work practice controls cannot reduce exposure to or below the PEL, the employer must include the use of appropriate respiratory protection in the written compliance program to achieve compliance with the PEL. This written program must be updated at least annually (more often, if necessary) and must be available for examination and copying to employees as well as the Assistant Secretary of Labor for Occupational Safety and Health and the Director of the National Institute for Occupational Safety and Health upon request.

A written compliance program must contain the following elements:

- A description of each operation that involves the emission of cadmium, the type of machinery used, the material processed, controls in place, and crew size.

- Description of operating and maintenance procedures and employee job responsibilities.

- Description of how the employer will achieve compliance, such as engineering plans and studies and the use of respiratory protection.

- A report on the technology used or considered for use to meet the PEL.

- Air monitoring data to document the sources of cadmium emissions.

- A schedule for implementation of the program that includes documentation such as copies of purchase orders for equipment and construction contracts.

- A plan for emergency situations that includes the use of respirators and personal protective equipment and methods to restrict access to an area to non-essential employees until the problem is corrected.

Requirements for protective equipment

Employees working in areas where exposure to cadmium is expected to exceed the PEL or where skin or eye irritation can result from cadmium exposure at any level must be provided with respiratory protection and other protective work clothing and equipment to prevent contamination of both the employee and the employee's clothes. If skin or eye irritation is associated with cadmium exposure at any level, the worker must be provided with equipment that protects the worker's skin and eyes. Examples of appropriate personal protective equipment include coveralls, gloves, head coverings, boots, face shields, and goggles. The employer must provide and maintain necessary personal protective equipment to employees at no cost and provide changing rooms, hand washing facilities, and showers.

The following precautions must be taken to protect workers:

- Employees must remove all protective work clothing and equipment at the end of a shift in a changing area designated for this purpose, taking care not to shake or blow any cadmium residue from the clothing or equipment.

- Changing rooms must have separate storage areas for street clothes and for cadmium-contaminated protective clothing.

- The employer must clean and maintain protective work clothing and equipment, which includes washing at least once a week and repairing or replacing as necessary; tears or rips in protective clothing must be repaired immediately or the item replaced.

- Employees exposed to cadmium above the PEL must shower at the end of a work shift when exposure occurred and may not eat, drink, smoke, chew tobacco or gum, or apply cosmetics before washing their hands and face.

Special cleaning requirements for protective clothing

Cleaning or laundering cadmium-contaminated work clothing requires special precautions. The employer must ensure that any person designated to handle protective clothing and equipment contaminated with cadmium understands the potential harmful effects of exposure and knows how to launder or clean such items in a safe manner that prevents the release of cadmium at levels above the PEL.

An important step in this process is to ensure that only authorized employees remove cadmium-contaminated clothing or equipment from the workplace for any purpose, including laundering, cleaning, or disposal. Items removed from the work area for cleaning, maintenance, or disposal must be placed in sealed, impermeable bags designed to prevent dispersion of cadmium dust. These bags must be labeled as described in the section on communicating hazards to employees.

Types of respirators

The respiratory protection program must comply with 29 CFR 1910.134 (Respiratory Protection), including the need for a written respiratory protection program administered by a trained administrator. Respirators must be used any time employees are exposed to cadmium at levels above the PEL, including maintenance and repair activities as well as normal operations.

The following table (page 13) depicts specific requirements for respirators, depending on the exposure level, but respirators assigned for higher environmental concentrations may be used at lower exposure levels. Quantitative fit testing is required for all tight-fitting air purifying respirators when the airborne concentration of cadmium exceeds 10 times the PEL. If there is any indication of eye irritation, a full face piece respirator is required.

Requirements for medical monitoring

The employer must institute a medical surveillance program for all employees who are or may be exposed to cadmium at or above the action level for 30 or more days per year (or in a 12-month consecutive period). All medical examinations related to this requirement must be provided at no cost to the employee at a reasonable time and convenient place, and they must be performed by or under the supervision of a licensed physician who is familiar with the regulatory text of the cadmium standard, including appendices that provide details on health effects and protocols for sample handling and laboratory selection. Biological samples must be collected in a manner that assures their reliability, and analyses must be performed in laboratories with demonstrated proficiency in the testing performed.

The employer must promptly inform the employee of the option to seek a second medical opinion after any medical examination or consultation provided by a physician provided by the employer to review any findings, determinations, or recommendations or to

Table 1: Respiratory Protection for Cadmium

Airborne Concentration	Required Respirator Type
Less than 10 times the PEL	A half mask, air purifying equipped with a high-efficiency particulate air (HEPA) filter.
Up to 25 times the PEL	A powered air-purifying respirator (PAPR) with a loose-fitting hood or helmet equipped with a HEPA filter or a supplied-air respirator with a loose-fitting hood or helmet face piece operated in the continuous flow mode.
Up to 50 times the PEL	A full face piece air-purifying respirator equipped with a HEPA filter or a powered air-purifying respirator with a tight-fitting half mask equipped with a HEPA filter or a supplied-air respirator with a tight-fitting half mask operated in the continuous flow mode
Up to 250 times the PEL	A powered air-purifying respirator with a tight fitting full face piece equipped with a HEPA filter or a supplied-air respirator with a tight-fitting full face piece operated in the continuous flow mode.
Up to 1,000 times the PEL	A supplied air respirator with half mask or full face piece operated in the pressure demand or other positive pressure mode.
More than 1,000 times the PEL or unknown levels of concentration	A self-contained breathing apparatus with a full face piece operated in the pressure demand or other positive pressure mode, or a supplied-air respirator with a full face piece operated in the pressure demand or other positive pressure mode and equipped with an auxiliary escape type self-contained breathing apparatus operated in the pressure demand mode.
Fire Fighting	A self-contained breathing apparatus with full face piece operated in the pressure demand or other positive pressure mode.

Source: Respiratory Decision Logic, NIOSH, 1987

conduct examinations, consultations, or laboratory tests. The employer may require the employee to notify the employee that he or she intends to seek a second medical opinion and to initiate steps to make an appointment within 15 days of being told of this option or of receiving the physician's written opinion from an employer-provided examination, whichever is later, as a condition of providing payment for a second medical opinion.

Medical surveillance begins with an initial examination for each employee covered by this requirement within 30 days of employment in a position that involves exposure to cadmium. The only exception is for employees who can show that they have had an examination that includes all required elements in the last 12 months. Results from a qualifying examination within the last 12 months must be maintained as part of the employee's medical record and are treated as the initial examination. The examination must include:

- Medical and work history
  - Any past, present, or anticipated future exposure to cadmium
  - History of renal, cardiovascular, respiratory, hematopoietic, reproductive or musculoskeletal system dysfunction
  - Current use of medication with potential nephrotoxic side effects
  - Smoking history and current status
- Biological monitoring
  - Cadmium in urine (CdU), standardized to grams of creatinine (g/Cr)
  - Beta-2 microglobulin in urine (β2-M), standardized to grams of creatinine (g/Cr), with pH specified
  - Cadmium in blood (CdB), standardized to liters of whole blood (lwb)

The following parameters will determine what level of medical surveillance will follow the initial examination. Levels at or below the levels specified below require only the minimum level of periodic medical surveillance, which includes a follow-up exam within one year of the initial exam and a periodic exam every two years from that point forward. Biological sampling must be provided at least annually.

Trigger levels for medical surveillance:

- CdU level: at or below 3 μg/g Cr
- β2-M level: at or below 300 μg/g Cr
- CdB level: at or below 5 μg/lwb

If the initial biological monitoring tests for an employee show levels exceeding any of the above parameters, then the employer must reassess the employee's occupational exposure to cadmium within two weeks of receiving the results of the tests. This reassessment must include a reevaluation and reassessment of the employee's work practices and personal hygiene, respirator use (if any) and respirator program, smoking history and current usage, as well as available hygiene facilities and engineering controls in use. If any deficiencies are noted during this reevaluation, the employer must correct them within 30 days.

An employee who shows biological test results elevated relative to the trigger levels noted above must receive a full medical examination within 90 days after receiving the results from the initial testing. At this point, the examining physician should make a decision whether to medically remove the employee from cadmium exposure. If the physician decides not to medically remove the employee, biological monitoring must continue on a semiannual basis along with an annual medical exam.

If an employee shows biological testing results during both the initial and follow-up medical examination elevated above the following trigger levels, that employee must be medically removed from exposure to cadmium at or above the action level:

(1) CdU level: above 7 μg/g Cr

    or

(2) CdB level: above 10 μg/liter of whole blood

    or

(3) β2-M level: above 750 μg/g Cr

    and

(a) CdU exceeds 3 µg/g Cr

   or

(b) CdB exceeds 5 µg/liter of whole blood

Employee removal is mandatory if the second set of biological monitoring results from the medical examination shows that one of the above mandatory removal trigger levels has been exceeded. The employer must continue to monitor the employee with biological monitoring on a quarterly basis along with semiannual medical examinations until such time as the employee's levels fall within the acceptable trigger levels for medical surveillance. Employee removal is also required if the examining physician determines that the employee needs removal from exposure to cadmium based on other findings from the examination regardless of the above testing results.

Required periodic medical exams

The minimum level of medical surveillance for employees who face exposure to cadmium but who do not test above trigger limits during biological sampling includes an exam within one year after the initial exam and thereafter an exam at least every two years. This exam must include the following:

- Detailed medical and work history.
- Complete physical examination, emphasizing blood pressure, the respiratory system, and the urinary system.
- A 14 x 17 inch or a reasonably-sized posterior-anterior chest x-ray (frequency to be determined by the examining physician).
- Pulmonary function tests.
- Blood analysis.
- Urinalysis.
- Prostate exam for males over 40 years old.
- Other tests deemed appropriate by the physician.

Annual biological sampling is required, either as part of the medical exam or separately as periodic biological monitoring. When an employee who has been previously provided with medical surveillance is terminated or voluntarily leaves employment, the employer must provide a medical examination that includes a chest x-ray. If the last periodic or other required exam was less than six months prior to the date of termination or departure, no further exam is required.

Access to and protection of medical information

The employer must provide the examining physician with a copy of the OSHA cadmium standard and all appendices, a description of each affected employee's former, current, and anticipated duties and exposure levels as they relate to the employee's occupational exposure to cadmium, results of any previous medical and biological monitoring, and a description of personal protective equipment used by each employee.

The employer shall obtain from the examining physician a written medical opinion for each medical examination performed on each employee. The physician must be told not to reveal any findings or diagnoses unrelated to occupational exposure to cadmium to the employer. The written opinion must include:

- A diagnosis for the employee.
- A written opinion as to whether the employee has any medical condition that places him or her at increased risk of material impairment to health from further exposure to cadmium, including evidence of cadmium toxicity.
- Results of biological tests.
- Any recommended removal from or limitation on the activities or duties of the employee, or on the employee's use of personal protective equipment, such as respirators.
- A statement that the physician has clearly and carefully explained the results of the medical examination to the employee, including results of biological tests.

A copy of this written opinion and the results of the biological monitoring tests (including an explanation of the results) must be provided to the employee within two weeks after the employer receives it. If the employee requests access to the information provided by the employer to the physician, this information must be provided within 30 days.

Exposures created through emergencies

In the case of an emergency that may result in acute cadmium exposure for an employee, the employer must provide a medical examination equivalent to the standard periodic medical exam as soon as possible, with special emphasis on the respiratory system, other organ systems considered appropriate by the examining physician, and monitoring for symptoms of overexposure.

Procedures to remove an employee from duty

The employer must temporarily remove any employee from work where there is excess exposure to cadmium if biological monitoring tests show that employee to have reached any specific trigger zones or on each occasion that a physician determines in a written medical opinion that the employee must be removed. The employer must place that employee in another position where exposure to cadmium is below the action level. If such a position is not immediately available, the employer must provide one as soon as it becomes available. An employee must also be removed from excess cadmium exposure if a physician recommends this action, which can be based on biological monitoring results, an employee's inability to wear a respirator, evidence of illness or other signs or symptoms of cadmium-related dysfunction, or any other reason deemed medically appropriate by the physician. Inability to wear a respirator requires removal of the employee from work where exposure to cadmium is above the PEL; any other reason for removal requires removal of the worker from work where exposure to cadmium is below the action level.

Follow-up biological monitoring must be provided for any employee removed from duty at least every three months with follow-up medical examination semiannually until the examining physician provides a written opinion that the employee may be returned to the former job status or that the employee must be permanently removed from excess cadmium exposure.

The employer must provide Medical Removal Protection Benefits (MRPB) for up to a maximum of 18 months to an employee each time the employee is temporarily medically removed from a position because of excess cadmium exposure.

This requires the employer to sustain the normal earnings, seniority, and all other employee rights and benefits, including the right to former job status during this period. In return, the employer may require the employee to participate in medical surveillance. If an employee is unable to return to the former position by the end of the 18-month period, the employer must provide the employee with a medical examination to obtain a final medical determination regarding whether the employee can return to the former position or needs permanent removal from excess cadmium exposure.

Recordkeeping requirements

There are three distinct types of records required for an employer who operates a facility with the potential for occupational exposure to cadmium: air monitoring, medical surveillance, and training records.

Air monitoring records

The record of air monitoring must include the following:

- The date, duration, and results of air monitoring tests, in terms of an 8-hour TWA for each sample.
- The name, social security number, and job classification of the employees monitored as well as all employees the monitoring is intended to represent.
- A description of the sampling and analytical methods used and evidence of their accuracy.
- The type, if any, of respiratory protection worn by the monitored employee(s).
- A notation of any conditions that may affect the outcome of the monitoring results.

The employer must maintain these records for 30 years.

The employer may use "objective data" as an exemption from the requirement for initial monitoring under the OSHA standard. OSHA defines "objective data" as "information demonstrating that a particular product or material containing cadmium or a specific process, operation, or activity involving cadmium cannot release dust or fumes in concentrations at or above the action level even under the worst-case release conditions." Such information may be obtained from industry wide studies or from laboratory test results conducted under conditions similar to those used by the employer in current operations. If the employer chooses to use objective data, records to substantiate this decision must be maintained for 30 years.

Medical surveillance records

The employer must maintain records for every employee subject to medical surveillance that includes the following:

- The name and social security number of the employee.
- A description of the employee's duties.
- A copy of the physician's written opinions and an explanation sheet for biological monitoring results.
- A copy of the medical history and results of the physical examination and all test results.
- A description of any employee symptoms that might be related to cadmium exposure.
- A copy of the information provided to the physician.

These records must be maintained for the duration of the employee's employment with the company plus 30 years. Upon request of the employee, an employee's designated representative, anyone having the written consent of the employee, and members of the employee's family after the employee's death or incapacitation, the employer must provide copies of these records within 15 days of such a request.

Training records

The employer must create a certification record showing that employees have been trained, to include the identity of the trained employee, the signature of the trainer or the employer, and the date the training was completed. These records must be retained for one year after the training.

If an employer ceases to do business and no successor employer is available to retain the records required to be maintained by the business, the employer must comply with the requirements for transferring records contained in 29 CFR 1910.1020 (h).

OSHA assistance

OSHA can provide extensive help through a variety of programs, including technical assistance about effective safety and health programs, state plans, workplace consultations, voluntary protection programs, strategic partnerships, and training and education, and more. An overall commitment to workplace safety and health can add value to your business, to your workplace, and to your life.

Safety and health program management guidelines

Effective management of worker safety and health protection is a decisive factor in reducing the extent and severity of work-related injuries and illnesses and their related costs. In fact, an effective safety and health program forms the basis of good worker protection and can save time and money (about $4 for every dollar spent) and increase productivity and reduce worker injuries, illnesses, and related workers' compensation costs.

To assist employers and employees in developing effective safety and health programs, OSHA published recommended Safety and Health Program Management Guidelines (54 Federal Register (16): 3904-3916, January 26, 1989). These voluntary guidelines can be applied to all places of employment covered by OSHA.

The guidelines identify four general elements critical to the development of a successful safety and health management system:

- Management leadership and employee involvement.
- Work analysis.
- Hazard prevention and control.
- Safety and health training.

The guidelines recommend specific actions, under each of these general elements, to achieve an effective safety and health program. The Federal Register notice is available online at www.osha.gov.

State programs

The Occupational Safety and Health Act of 1970 (OSH Act) encourages states to develop and operate their own job safety and health plans. OSHA approves and monitors these plans. There are currently 26 state plans: 23 cover both private and public (state and local government) employment; 3 states, Connecticut, New Jersey, and New York, cover the public sector only. States and territories with their own OSHA-approved occupational safety and health plans must adopt standards identical to, or at least as effective as, the Federal standards.

Consultation services

Consultation assistance is available on request to employers who want help in establishing and maintaining a safe and healthful workplace. Largely funded by OSHA, the service is provided at no cost to the employer. Primarily developed for smaller employers with more hazardous operations, the consultation service is delivered by state governments employing professional safety and health consultants. Comprehensive assistance includes an appraisal of all-mechanical systems, work practices, and occupational safety and health hazards of the workplace and all aspects of the employer's present job safety and health program. In addition, the service offers assistance to employers in developing and implementing an effective safety and health program. No penalties are proposed or citations issued for hazards identified by the consultant. OSHA provides consultation assistance to the employer with the assurance that his or her name and firm and any information about the workplace will not be routinely reported to OSHA enforcement staff.

Under the consultation program, certain exemplary employers may request participation in OSHA's Safety and Health Achievement Recognition Program (SHARP). Eligibility for participation in SHARP includes receiving a comprehensive consultation visit, demonstrating exemplary achievements in workplace safety and health by abating all identified hazards, and developing an excellent safety and health program.

Employers accepted into SHARP may receive an exemption from programmed inspections (not complaint or accident investigation inspections) for a period of 1 year. For more information concerning consultation assistance, visit OSHA's website at www.osha.gov.

Voluntary Protection Programs (VPP)

Voluntary Protection Programs and onsite consultation services, when coupled with an effective enforcement program, expand worker protection to help meet the goals of the OSH Act. The three levels of VPP are Star, Merit, and Demonstration designed to recognize outstanding achievements by companies that have successfully incorporated comprehensive safety and health programs into their total management system. The VPP motivate others to achieve excellent safety and health results in the same outstanding way as they establish a cooperative relationship between employers, employees, and OSHA.

For additional information on VPP and how to apply, contact the OSHA regional offices listed at the end of this publication.

Strategic Partnership Program

OSHA's Strategic Partnership Program, the newest member of OSHA's cooperative programs, helps encourage, assist, and recognize the efforts of partners to eliminate serious workplace hazards and achieve a high level of worker safety and health. Whereas OSHA's Consultation Program and VPP entail one-on-one relationships between OSHA and individual work sites, most strategic partnerships seek to have a broader impact by building cooperative relationships with groups of employers and employees. These partnerships are voluntary, cooperative relationships between OSHA, employers, employee representatives, and others (e.g., trade unions, trade and professional associations, universities, and other government agencies).

For more information on this and other cooperative programs, contact your nearest OSHA office, or visit OSHA's website at www.osha.gov.

Alliance Programs

Alliances enable organizations committed to workplace safety and health to collaborate with OSHA to prevent injuries and illnesses in the workplace. OSHA and its allies work together to reach out to, educate, and lead the nation's employers and their employees in improving and advancing workplace safety and health.

Alliances are open to all, including trade or professional organizations, businesses, labor organizations, educational institutions, and government agencies. In some cases, organizations may be building on existing relationships with OSHA through other cooperative programs.

There are few formal program requirements for alliances, which are less structured than other cooperative agreements, and the agreements do not include an enforcement component. However, OSHA and the participating organizations must define, implement, and meet a set of short- and long-term goals that fall into three categories: training and education; outreach and communication; and promotion of the national dialogue on workplace safety and health.

OSHA training and education

OSHA area offices offer a variety of information services, such as compliance assistance, technical advice, publications, audiovisual aids and speakers for special engagements. OSHA's Training Institute in Arlington Heights, IL, provides basic and advanced courses in safety and health for federal and state compliance officers, state consultants, federal agency personnel, and private sector employers, employees, and their representatives.

The OSHA Training Institute also has established OSHA Training Institute Education Centers to address the increased demand for its courses from the private sector and from other Federal agencies.

These centers are nonprofit colleges, universities, and other organizations that have been selected after a competition for participation in the program.

OSHA also provides funds to nonprofit organizations, through grants, to conduct workplace training and education in subjects where OSHA believes there is a lack of workplace training. Grants are awarded annually. Grant recipients are expected to contribute 20 percent of the total grant cost.

For more information on grants, training, and education, contact the OSHA Training Institute, Office of Training and Education, 2020 South Arlington Heights Rd., Arlington Heights, IL 60005, (847) 297-4810. For further information on any OSHA program, contact your nearest OSHA area or regional office listed at the end of this publication.

Information available electronically

OSHA has a variety of materials and tools available on its website at www.osha.gov. These include e-Tools such as Expert Advisors, Electronic Compliance Assistance Tools (e-cats), Technical Links; regulations, directives, publications; videos, and other information for employers and employees. OSHA's software programs and compliance assistance tools walk you through challenging safety and health issues and common problems to find the best solutions for your workplace.

OSHA's CD-ROM includes standards, interpretations, directives, and more and can be purchased on CD-ROM from the U.S. Government Printing Office. To order, write to the Superintendent of Documents, P.O. Box 371954, Pittsburgh, PA 15250-7954 or phone (202) 512-1800, or order online at http://bookstore.gpo.gov.

OSHA publications

OSHA has an extensive publications program. For a listing of free or sales items, visit OSHA's website at www.osha.gov or contact the OSHA Publications Office, U.S. Department of Labor, 200 Constitution Avenue, NW, N-3101, Washington, DC 20210. Telephone (202) 693-1888 or fax to (202) 693-2498.

Contacting OSHA

To report an emergency, file a complaint, or seek OSHA advice, assistance, or products, call (800) 321-OSHA or contact your nearest OSHA regional or area office listed at the end of this publication. The teletypewriter (TTY) number is (877) 889-5627.

You can also file a complaint online and obtain more information on OSHA federal and state programs by visiting OSHA's website at www.osha.gov.

For more information on grants, training, and education, contact the OSHA Training Institute, Office of Training and Education, 2020 South Arlington Heights Rd., Arlington Heights, IL 60005, (847) 297-4810, or see "Outreach" on OSHA's website at www.osha.gov.

OSHA Regional Offices

Region I
(CT,* ME, MA, NH, RI, VT*)
Boston, MA 02203
(617) 565-9860

Region II
(NJ,* NY,* PR,* VI*)
201 Varick Street, Room 670
New York, NY 10014
(212) 337-2378

Region III
(DE, DC, MD,* PA,* VA,* WV)
The Curtis Center
170 S. Independence Mall West
Suite 740 West
Philadelphia, PA 19106-3309
(215) 861-4900

Region IV
(AL, FL, GA, KY,* MS, NC,*
SC,* TN*)
Atlanta Federal Center
61 Forsyth Street SW, Room 6T50
Atlanta, GA 30303
(404) 562-2300

Region V
(IL, IN,* MI,* MN,* OH, WI)
230 South Dearborn Street
Room 3244
Chicago, IL 60604
(312) 353-2220

Region VI
(AR, LA, NM,* OK, TX)
525 Griffin Street, Room 602
Dallas, TX 75202
(214) 767-4731 or 4736 x224

Region VII
(IA,* KS, MO, NE)
City Center Square
1100 Main Street, Suite 800
Kansas City, MO 64105
(816) 426-5861

Region VIII
(CO, MT, ND, SD, UT,* WY*)
1999 Broadway, Suite 1690
P.O. Box 46550
Denver, CO 80202-5716
(303) 844-1600

Region IX
(American Samoa, AZ,* CA,* HI,
NV,* Northern Mariana Islands)
71 Stevenson Street, Room 420
San Francisco, CA 94105
(415) 975-4310

Region X
(AK,* ID, OR,* WA*)
1111 Third Avenue, Suite 715
Seattle, WA 98101-3212
(206) 553-5930

*These states and territories operate their own OSHA-approved job safety and health programs (Connecticut, New Jersey, and New York plans cover public employees only). States with approved programs must have a standard that is identical to, or at least as effective as, the Federal standard.

Note: Please visit www.OSHA.gov or call (800) 321-OSHA for information on OSHA area offices, OSHA-approved state plans, and OSHA consultation projects.